TORVILL AND DEAN

F*I*R*E O*N I*C*E

TORVILL AND DEAN

F*I*R*E   O*N   I*C*E

JAYNE TORVILL AND CHRISTOPHER DEAN
WITH NEIL WILSON
PHOTOGRAPHS BY BOB MARTIN

Weidenfeld and Nicolson
London

P*R*E*F*A*C*E

During the last few weeks, the question everybody has asked has been why we chose to pit ourselves again against the best amateur ice dancers in the world. Were our achievements before, all the medals and the acclaim, not enough for any two people in one lifetime?

The answer is, simply, the challenge. It is that which has been behind everything we have ever done, whether it was amateur sport, professional competitions or commercial shows. It is what has driven us, what has made it all worthwhile. And what bigger challenge could there have been than coming back into the Olympic arena ten years after we walked out of it for what we thought would be the last time?

For years we have enjoyed artistic freedom, a licence denied those in most sports. We could skate to our hearts' content. We were our own bosses. We could rehearse when we wanted, where we wanted. Any music, any dance, just as long as it pleased us and an audience.

Now we're restricted again. There are rules we must follow, areas we cannot enter. Before we do anything, we have to ask our trainers Betty Callaway and Bobby Thompson whether it is allowed. And, worst of all, there is getting up in the morning again before seven to drive a long way to

THE COMEBACK
We decided to return to our roots. We took advantage of an invitation to professional skaters from the International Skating Union to return to our competitions, and prepared for one more season. Our first amateur performance after ten years was at the British Championships in Sheffield in January 1994.

A Love Story
With the melodramtic love story of Mack Sennett and Mabel Normand we managed to reach a public beyond ice dancing, even though the Broadway show from which we borrowed the idea bombed and was pulled off after nine days.

a public rink that is willing to give us the time to practise before it opens its doors to the public.

No matter what the results, the challenge has been worth it: it is an adventure. New music to be chosen, new steps to be choreographed and learned, new costumes to be designed and made. A new role to be played.

Life is too short to be still. We've been asked a thousand times since Sarajevo to dance Bolero, or Barnum, or Mack and Mabel. But our favourite routine, our favourite piece of music, is always the one we are working on at the time. That's the challenge.

How do we come up with the routines? Usually when we're not thinking about it. Most of the music we have used has been heard when we were not looking for anything, and it stuck in our minds. Let's Face the Music and Dance, which we used this winter as our free programme, was an idea ages before we thought about trying for the Olympics again.

This book covers our skating lives from the early days, and there are pictures within it we're embarrassed to look at now. But they are a part of the story, part of what we are and what we have done. They bring back memories. We hope they will for you.

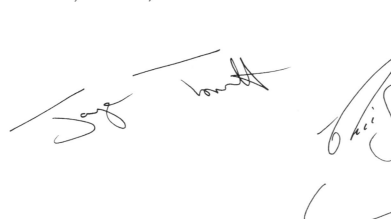

T·O·R·V·I·L·L
A·N·D
D·E·A·N

Torvill and Dean. Two names for one word in the mind of anyone who has ever seen them perform. A brand name for perfection. It has become a cliché, a word for the sublime blend of artistry to which every journalist and commentator retreats as the only description worthy of the performances, sporting or theatrical, that an extraordinary couple from Nottingham have given the world. Their names, wrote one admirer, go together like love and marriage, but those can be separable; you could have one without the other. But Torvill and Dean are one, two names so indivisible in the public mind that you can't imagine one without the other.

There was a time, of course, when their names weren't heard outside an inner-city ice rink in Nottingham, but now it would be enough in the British Isles to talk of Jayne and Chris for introductions to be unnecessary. Even beyond their native land they are known, probably because they have drawn admiring crowds in places where the only ice clinks in glasses.

INSPIRATION
Barnum was an idea that came to Chris as he watched the Moscow State Circus. He had swapped a ticket for the Bolshoi Ballet with another skater.

Torvill and Dean are everywhere synonymous with a degree of excellence so rare that it is hard to think of its like. Rolls and Royce, perhaps. Astaire and Rogers, Fonteyn and Nureyev? All are so immaculately matched and so finely in tune with each other that they have reached heights that are the stuff of legend.

Whether what Torvill and Dean did was ever merely sport has been the cause of much debate. That they extended the concept of sporting competition far beyond the common boundaries of the arena is unquestionable; they painted indelible pictures in the mind's eye that will linger long after the results are forgotten.

Their record as sporting competitors speaks for itself. Pure gold. In their earlier incarnation, they won six British championships, three European and four world titles, and on a magical evening in Sarajevo in the former republic of Yugoslavia they were crowned Olympic champions.

'The greatest ice dancers ever', was the opinion of

Lawrence Demmy, himself a former world champion, who was to become the sport's foremost international official. Statistically, his statement cannot be in dispute. They achieved a standard unlikely ever to be equalled. Maximum scores of sixes in every element of the sport, more than a hundred and fifty during their career. In the Olympic free-dance programme in Sarajevo they were awarded the highest score recorded in the sport of figure skating: 107.4 out of a possible total of 108 – a world record that still stands today.

So great were their sporting achievements that they came to transcend sport. BBC Television's Nine O'Clock News, an institution, was rescheduled to accommodate their performances, as was the printing of newspapers. They were honoured in the highest quarters, with MBEs by the Queen at Buckingham Palace and receptions at 10 Downing Street. Recently they were also given honorary Master of Arts degrees from Nottingham Trent University. T & D entered the language as an acronym.

But sport was limiting to them. The rules and restrictions that are a necessary element of all competition was frustrating. They had stretched the rules where they could – a lift here, a flip-over there – but there was only so much that could be achieved within the four minutes the sport allowed them. Dean, the great innovator, wanted more.

While the sporting world was still buzzing with the beauty of Bolero, they finally took their leave and set off on another challenging journey as professional performers, innovators still, but in the broader arena where applause and the box office are the final arbiters of success.

Now they are back, challenged by a rule change to become competitors again on the Olympic stage, and it is as if nothing has changed. The years just fell away; the decade disappeared as if a single moment. They are as good as ever, the unique partnership is as close as it ever was. You notice it wherever they are – on the practice rink, in the press conferences where they speak as if with one mind. Most of all, however, you notice it when they perform. As soon as the music starts to play they are not two individuals, but a single movement, blending into each other, flowing, fluid, in unison.

MACK AND MABEL REVISITED
When we turned professional, we were constantly asked to perform routines that we did as amateur competitors

Physically, they are ideal – Jayne is little more than a hundred pounds and small and Chris close to six feet tall, slender but powerful about the shoulders, able to twist and turn her, lift and launch her on a sheet of sheer ice with an effortless ease that defies belief.

The data does not exist that could find and match two

people so compatible as partners, and yet, in a city no bigger than Nottingham, chance brought them together when an instructor trying to place Chris with another girl came across Jayne's name as a skater who was unattached. Nothing before then had directed them towards each other. Chris was a successful ice dancer as a teenager and had another partner. Jayne had never even considered ice dancing, preferring the more acrobatic discipline of pairs skating, for which her smallness was a distinct advantage, and she had been a British junior champion.

Yet early one morning, at the invitation of an instructor at the Nottingham rink and so early in the day that Jayne admits having been bleary so with sleep that she can remember little of it, there began a partnership that was blessed. How else can you explain why the phone call that was to team them with Betty Callaway, their trainer, came to be made right when she was contemplating a letter announcing the retirement of another couple she trained, a letter that turned out to have been a misunderstanding? She was the catalyst of the team that gathered around Torvill and Dean, people like Courtney Jones, a former world champion ice dancer, and Bobby Thompson, a trainer. Each had an understanding of ice dancing and the ability to enhance Chris's creativity as a choreographer.

So many more contributed – dressmakers, ballet dancers, musicians, arrangers. Their parents, certainly, and Debbie Turner, an admirer who became their faithful personal assistant, smoothing their professional path and clearing the way for their return to amateur sport. All have played a part, and Jayne and Chris played theirs. For all of them, and their audiences, it has been a fantastic adventure. This is its story.

A TORVILL AND DEAN CLASSIC
For the original set pattern section in 1982 we did a blues to Larry Adler's haunting rendition of *Summertime.*

CHAPTER ONE

1975 - 81

E·A·R·L·Y
Y·E·A·R·S

The working partnership that became the most famous in ice skating began at the Thursday evening dance class at Nottingham Ice Rink, and not auspiciously. If any who were there now say that they saw what might one day be, their memory deceives them: Jayne fell in a blues number, hitting her head and elbow.

It was hardly surprising. A pairs skater who had tasted success, she competed at the European Championships at the age of fourteen. She had tried ice dancing years earlier but long forgotten the steps she was taught, and there were many she had never learned. She was there only because Chris and his partner, with whom he had won the British

Primary Championships, had a falling out. Jayne might not have been the obvious choice, but having lost her pairs partner to another girl, she was unattached – and willing.

Janet Sawbridge, a former British champion at both pairs and dance and a new instructor at Nottingham, sized them up, liked what she found and put them together. Under her teaching, they developed so well in four months that in their first competition together they were second.

Those who knew them say that they were a shy pair, but they lived close to each other, she above her parents' newsagent's shop and he a few streets away. They became friends and their partnership evolved. A local competition at Sheffield brought them their first victory, and eleven months after teaming up they became Northern champions.

Their skating now occupied every spare hour – two hours every day, sometimes four, and always three hours on Sundays. But there were failures on the way. The first time they took the National Skating Association's test, which would qualify them to compete in the National Championships, Chris failed. They passed after a second attempt, but the partnership was strained by other demands. Chris, a police cadet, had to attend a police college in Yorkshire. He could train only at weekends, and the double life was tiring him. More than once he told Jayne to find another partner, but she would not hear of it, fetching him before dawn and driving from places up to forty-five minutes away to keep him in training.

JAYNE MIGHT NOT HAVE BEEN THE OBVIOUS CHOICE, BUT WAS UNATTACHED — AND WILLING.

Her perseverance paid off. They won their first international competition in St Gervais, Switzerland, and their second in Oberstdorf, an Alpine resort in Bavaria that was to become their training base. In 1977 they won selection for the 1978 European and World Championships. They were on the main highway to success, but the journey's destination was far from view: they were ninth at the Europeans, eleventh at the Worlds.

THEY WON THEIR FIRST INTERNATIONAL COMPETITION IN ST GERVAIS.

Not everything went smoothly. On their return from the World Championships they learned that Janet Sawbridge was expecting a baby and had decided to give up teaching. They would have to find a new trainer.

Many were considered, but all were too far from Nottingham, where Chris was tied to his police duties and Jayne to a job in insurance. Then the manager of the Nottingham rink suggested Betty Callaway, a former professional skater who had trained a German couple to the European title and was helping a Hungarian couple, Krisztina Regoeczy and Andras Sallay. He made contact with her, put the question, and the timing turned out to be perfect.

Callaway had received a letter from Hungary that she understood to mean that Regoeczy and Sallay were retiring. Free of commitments – she thought – she agreed to spend each weekend with Torvill and Dean at Nottingham for little more than her expenses. They would be her first British couple. It would be an interesting challenge. Then came the news that the Hungarians never intended to retire. The

**NOTTINGHAM
ICE RINK**
Nottingham Ice Rink
was our first home,
where one early morn-
ing we were brought
together as ice
dancers. But the
hours when we could
use the rink were
uncivilized, the ice
often crowded, and
as soon as we climbed
a few rungs on the
ladder we sought sanc-
tuary in quieter rinks
in Switzerland and
Germany.

letter had been misinterpreted, but Betty refused to go back on her agreement, and a deal was agreed whereby the Hungarians would train on weekdays with Betty in Richmond, where they would be her priority, and at weekends all three would commute to Notting-ham to join Chris and Jayne. It worked. Both couples were to become world champions.

The winter of 1979/80 Jayne and Chris improved to sixth in the European Championships and eighth in the Worlds. They were making strides and becoming noticed. Advice was offered and accepted from many wishing to see them suc-ceed. Lawrence Demmy suggested to Betty that Jayne should project herself more, change her hairstyle and wear less subtle make-up. Zoltan Nagy, a Hungarian ballet dancer who accompanied Regoeczy and Sallay abroad, helped Chris on his moves, and their choice of routines and music matured.

There are three elements in ice-dancing competition: compulsory dances, comprising two sections in which each couple perform the same routine to the same music – such as blues, paso doble or rumba – are the least rewarding both to the skaters and their marks. Betty was acknowledged mis-tress of these. In the second, skaters choose their own music and original dance to a specified rhythm. In the finale there is a free choice of music, rhythm and routine, so originality and creativity are important – Chris's forte.

For the 1980/81 season, he chose *On a Little Street in Singapore* for their original dance, a foxtrot, and introduced jazz to ice dancing with a combination of Glen Miller's *In the Mood* and Benny Goodman's *Swing, Swing, Swing*. The judges approved. At the European Championships in Gothenburg they were awarded eleven marks of 5.7 and finished fourth. At the Winter Olympic Games in Lake Placid they were fifth and were back to fourth at the World Championships.

Their accession came sooner than expected: the next winter. Both were totally committed now, having given up their jobs, and they were dependent on a generous yearly grant of £14,000 from Nottingham City Council. It paid early dividends.

For that season they chose *Cherry Pink and Apple Blossom White* for the required cha-cha original, and a selection with a rock-'n'-roll flavour for the free. It was their compulsories, however, that sent them on course for their dramatic first victory in February 1981 at the European Championships in Innsbruck – they were first in all. They stayed first after the original, but narrowly; the free would be decisive. Immediately behind them were the new Olympic champions and a couple who were formerly world champions. Torvill and Dean had to be at their best, and they were. Seven of the nine judges placed them first.

Four weeks later they were world champions. All nine judges placed them first after the original dance, all nine awarded them 5.9 for their free programme. The succession had been decided, the new king and queen of ice dance crowned.

IN THE MOOD

For our first Olympic season, we took jazz as our theme – Glenn Miller's *In the Mood* and Benny Goodman's *Swing, Swing, Swing* – it worked for us immediately. When we debuted in London, we were able to beat our Hungarian training partners, Krisztina Regoeczy and Andras Sallay, who also worked with Betty Callaway and who became world champions later that season. We were satisfied by our improvement to fifth place at the Olympics at Lake Placid, but the main jubilation in the British camp was over the victory of the Bristol figure skater Robin Cousins in the men's event.

THE WESTMINSTER WALTZ

The Westminster Waltz at the 1981 European Championships in Innsbruck, the first of four compulsory dances there, was a milestone for us. For the first time the judges placed us number one, ahead of the previous year's Olympic champions. We were surprised by the results because three of the couples ahead of us the year before were still competing. We stayed first after a paso doble, rumba and cha-cha, and over the next four years of competition we always managed to be first in compulsories.

WORLD CHAMPIONS FOR THE FIRST TIME

We won our first European and World titles in 1981 to a routine that began with jazz music from *Fame*, changed into an Eygptian theme with *Caravan*, slowed to a seductive rumba from *Red Sails in the Sunset* and finished with *Swing, Swing, Swing*. It was the last time we stitched music together in that fashion but it worked. Seven of the nine judges at the Europeans placed us first and an eighth first equal. Only one Russian judge voted for a Russian couple, Irina Moiseyeva and Andrei Minenko, former world champions. A few weeks later, in Hartford, Connecticut, our marks rose higher, the Russians slipped, and we became world champions for the first time.

CHAPTER TWO

1982

M·A·C·K

A·N·D

M·A·B·E·L

Torvill and Dean were world champions now, but for how long? The old order had been swept away, but there were new challengers appearing from the Soviet Union and the United States. Many, even among their British admirers, feared that they had peaked too early in the four-year cycle that leads to the ultimate competition, the Olympic Games.

Each season demands something fresh – new costumes, new music, new routines – and if they were to defend the reputation established in 1981, they had to be different. What to do next was a thought even before the last season had ended.

As so often, they found the answer in an idea that had occurred to them as a possibility years earlier

**I WON'T SEND
ROSES**
(Preceding pages) We
performed a special
section of Mack and
Mabel at the Rich-
mond gala in 1982.
This is the final pose.

ACCOLADES
We were proud to
receive a number of
honours after the tri-
umphs of 1981. Prime
Minister Margaret
Thatcher attended a
gala in Richmond,
and she invited us to
10 Downing Street.
The city council in
our home town of
Nottingham, which
supported us finan-
cially, also conferred
on us the freedom of
the city.

and been consigned to the back of their minds. In one of
their periodic visits to the library of their local radio station
in Nottingham, they found a recording of a Broadway show.
Called *Mack and Mabel*, the show had been a flop, closing after
nine days. But they liked its overture, and Chris saw possibili-
ties in the melodramatic story of a love affair between the
silent-movie star Mack Sennett and
his leading lady, Mabel Normand.

Most free dances are a potpourri
of music spliced together to give
four minutes of various styles and
tempos. Chris had it in his mind to
offer a single piece telling a whole
story, lifted almost intact from the
overture. Ice dancing had never
seen its like, and it might have
challenged the natural conser-
vatism of the judges, but Chris set
about creating a cameo that would tell of a dramatic love
affair through to its climactic ending.

The other choice to be made was the original dance. The
International Skating Union had dictated that it should be a
blues that season, and that brought to their mind an edition
of a chat show in which Larry Adler performed on his har-
monica the old Gershwin standard, *Summertime*. The ISU's
rules allow a range of tempos, and Chris chose the slowest,
emphasizing its sombre, haunting appeal to create a soulful
routine.

The work on both was done in Oberstdorf. Sometimes

Betty would be with them, and they went for help on per-fecting the dances to Michael Stylianos, a former Latin American ballroom world champion whose advice they had sought on their cha-cha the previous year. But the dances remained their own creation, every step calculated and pol-ished to their own rising standards. Some steps followed a natural progression; others offered themselves by chance. The scissor steps in Mack and Mabel, which were to become famous, came about when they were playing around without

EVERY STEP WAS CALCULATED AND POLISHED TO THEIR OWN RISING STANDARDS.

the music, unable to synchronize their steps. In the mirror they happened to catch the effect of the move, and it was incorporated into the piece.

There were other innovations. One was an unusual move in which Chris lifted Jayne under her shoulder blades and twisted her to bring them face to face before returning her to the ice. Another had Jayne throwing herself on Chris's hip, from which he twirled her horizontally. The ice-dancing world was to see a revolution, but would it be welcome?

The public premiere of the new routine was at an event at the Richmond rink in west London. There were none of the potential international challengers to beat, but its reception by the audience as well as the judges was crucial. Word can spread quickly in the small world of ice dancing, and judges can be influenced by good reports from others. They could not have hoped for more than they were to receive that evening. Summertime received one six, an uncommon mark for an original dance, and Mack and Mabel won sixes from a Canadian, an Austrian and, significantly, a Russian judge.

The next test was the British Championships at their home rink in Nottingham, which presented a special kind of pressure. There was no doubt that they would win; there were only six competitors. But how comfortably?

They need not have worried. Sixes were becoming the hallmark of their performances. All nine judges awarded them sixes for artistic impression, and seven of them the maximum score again for technical merit. The reaction, at the rink and from the audience on television, was ecstatic.

Suddenly, Torvill and Dean were more popular in Britain than their sport. The country was going through a difficult time economically, and they lifted everyone's spirits. They were British and the best. A week later, when they took the National Skating Association's gold-star test, normally a private occasion attended only by judges and the press, a thousand spectators greeted them.

SIXES WERE BECOMING THE HALLMARK OF THEIR PERFORMANCES.

The European Championships in Lyon, France, followed, and again Torvill and Dean triumphed. The judges seemed convinced that here was a couple who could raise the discipline to greater heights, and they fell over each other to heap the honours upon them. They were marked first by every judge on each compulsory dance, with second places going to a Russian couple, Natalia Bestemianova and Andre Bukin. Summertime confirmed their preeminence, and the French crowd broke into applause that threatened to drown the music on their final circuit. All around the rink people were in tears of emotion, and their reward was three pairs of sixes, the perfect score of twelve.

It was not over yet. The Russians could still win by taking the free programme, and they drew to skate first. They scored six 5.9s and nothing below 5.7, but it was a hopeless task because the judges held back, leaving room on their scorecards for what they knew was to come. Jayne and Chris

ALL AROUND THE RINK PEOPLE WERE IN TEARS OF EMOTION.

got three sixes for technical merit and eight for artistic impression, a total of eleven – and a record at the time for an international championship.

At the World Championships in Copenhagen, they skated Summertime even better, the best ever, they both believe. This time they were awarded six sixes, and after Mack and Mabel the Brondby-Hallen rink was a field of flowers. They were world champions again, and for years ice dancing would not be the same. They had changed its character. Bernard Ford, a former world champion, put it perfectly: 'It's like watching God skate.'

MEN WITH TEARS
If our victory at the 1981 World Championships surprised the world of ice dancing, Mack and Mabel, our free dance, must have seemed revolutionary. But it was our programme for *Summertime* that set the tone. After we skated it at the 1982 European Championships in Lyon, we were told that there were men watching with tears in their eyes.

SIXES ON AN ORIGINAL DANCE

At the European Championships we received three sixes for artistic impression, the first we'd been awarded for an original dance, but the record lasted only a few weeks: at the World Championships, six judges awarded us sixes for artistic impression. A French woman liked it enough to give us a six twice, a first for an original dance.

A ROMANCE OF PURE MELODRAMA
Mack and Mabel was the story of the silent-movie
star Mack Sennett and the stormy love affair with
his leading lady, Mabel Normand. Chris took the
music from the overture to the Broadway show
and wove around it a romance of pure melodrama: the tale of a rejected woman tossed away by
her man and her attempts to win him back.

CHANGING TEMPO
We used all four minutes allowed for our free
programme, which in itself started a trend in the
sport. Here Jayne has thrown herself backwards
onto Chris's knee, signalling a change in the
piece's tempo.

PURE GOLD

Though Mack and Mabel bombed on stage, it created history on ice for us. Part of its success were our matching eye-catching gold costumes, a one-button gold tuxedo with bow tie for Chris and a simple dress adorned by feathers for Jayne. At the World Championships in Copenhagen we had a near disaster when Chris's tuxedo button came unbuttoned and threatened to interfere with the routine.

AN AVALANCHE OF BOUQUETS
When we finished Mack and Mabel at the European Championships in Lyons, there was an avalanche of bouquets, ovations and sixes – eleven out of a possible eighteen.

AN EYE FOR FASHION
It was Courtney Jones, a former world ice dance champion and friend, who came up with the costume design. He used to skate around the practice rink behind us holding a tailor's chalk to make adjustments to the line and fitting. Detail was important to us, so everyone around us paid attention to every aspect of our performances.

CHAPTER THREE

1 9 8 3

B*A*R*N*U*M

After every World Championship, the International Skating Union invites the champions and other medallists on a world tour. It is hard work for little reward, but it is expected as a gesture to the sport. In 1982, though, it offered Jayne and Chris an unexpected bonus.

On a trip to Moscow for three days, some of the skaters were given tickets to the Bolshoi Ballet for one free evening. Chris was among them, and since ballet was a great love of his, he would normally have jumped at the chance. Instead, he had his mind set on something else, and he exchanged his ticket with a Canadian skater who had been invited to the Moscow State Circus.

There was a good reason. He was already thinking ahead to the next great challenge, and the circus had occurred to him as a possibility, full as it was of so many different movements, jugglers, trapeze artists, clowns and the music. The idea grew on him when he picked up a tape of Barnum, then a hit on Broadway and in London's West End. It happened to be a French-language version, but what mattered was the music and its appeal. Immediately he booked tickets for the show at the London Palladium for Jayne and himself.

They were recognized faces now, and spotted in the audience by the show's star, Michael Crawford, they were invited backstage. Could they use the music for their next routine, they asked. No problem, he said. But there was: vocals are banned from ice dancing, and there was no purely orchestral recording. Crawford came up with the solution, recruiting Michael Reed, the show's musical director. He put the music to piano, then brought musicians into a studio to record the full work — the first time music had been recorded to ice dancers' own specifications. They were leading the way once again.

Their original dance that year was rock 'n' roll. Again they happened upon an idea for the routine while sitting in a theatre. This time they were watching Andrew Lloyd Webber's *Song and Dance,*

OBERSTDORF

Not a fall on the ice but a roll in the snow. The work of creating and perfecting our routines was done each autumn in the Bavarian town of Oberstdorf, a place where we could relax away from the pressure of public and media attention at home. We chose it originally because the Nottingham rink closed for repairs at a critical time in our preparation, but the benefits of Oberstdorf drew us back year after year.

near the end of which the ballet dancer Wayne Sleep performs a rock sequence based on the music of Paganini. It was different. They seized on it.

The problem then became keeping the new dance and, more importantly, Barnum to themselves. Everybody now waited on them. What Torvill and Dean would do as an encore to last year's triumphs was a subject of concern to their competitors and of great interest to the British public.

THEY KEPT THE ROUTINE UNDER WRAPS, AND THE EVENING OF THE EVENT WAS HEAVY WITH EXPECTATION.

Revealed too soon it would lose its impact, a point that Chris always bore in mind as inveterate showman. So that winter they declined invitations to compete in the season's events, agreeing only to skate an exhibition at a London gala in which the audience had to be content with a reprise of Mack and Mabel. Only on the eve of the British Championships in Nottingham, at a press conference indicative of the public interest they now aroused, did they reveal their plan. Even the London correspondent of a Moscow newspaper appeared.

The story of Crawford's close involvement was told, but he was still one of the few who had actually seen the work performed. Even at the final official practice in Nottingham with judges present they kept it under wraps, and the evening of the event was heavy with expectation.

First, though, came the original. They wore simple white T-shirts, adorned only with the initials CJ, she with a black dress underneath and he with black trousers, both wearing a red scarf around their necks. They were rewarded for the dance with two sixes.

What followed was altogether different, a hilarious interpretation of a full circus show, with tightrope walking, clowning and a marching band. Both were in shiny white, accented by bright blue sashes and facings, and in an instant the ice rink became a sawdust ring, and everybody was transported into the Big Top. It was fun, it was clever, and it was a winner. A small trip flawed it, but every mark was 5.9 except a single six.

Incredibly, they were unhappy with the performance. Revisions were made – a more daring lift was added and a cartwheel dropped – and while practising the lift Jayne fell badly on her side and shoulder. No bones were broken but she was off the ice for days, and when she returned she fell again on the same lift. Hardly able to move her arm now, she was forced to withdraw them from the forthcoming European Championships.

Not until two weeks before the World Championships in Helsinki were they able to practise their routines again in full, and even then they avoided the more energetic sections of the rock 'n' roll dance to safeguard Jayne's arm. Betty,

IT WAS FUN, IT WAS CLEVER, AND IT WAS A WINNER.

however, revealed that she knew two weeks before Helsinki that they were ready. 'On this occasion they could do no wrong', she recalled. 'It was perfect, perfect. I don't think that Chris and Jayne even took one breath that was slightly different to the other's.'

They were as good as new once the competition began. An unprecedented row of 5.9s for one compulsory greeted their return, even though Jayne was skating with strapping around her shoulder, evident beneath her T-shirt when they performed the rock 'n' roll. But if the bandage affected her, it did not detract from her performance, and the judges bestowed fresh honours – another seven sixes.

Nothing prepared the Finnish audience for what was to come next. They skated Barnum to perfection. The crowd stood to them as one, showering the ice with bouquets and toys. Nine 5.9s for technical merit flashed first onto the scoreboard, followed immediately by nine sixes. Jayne let loose an ear-splitting shriek of excitement; beside them, Crawford punched the air.

THREE MINDS, ONE THOUGHT
At the practice rink in Oberstdorf, our trainer Betty Callaway talks over the morning's workout. Continually looking for improvement, we were never satisfied with what we had – we were always evolving.

Over the three sections of the competition – the compulsories, original and free – they averaged a mark of slightly more than 5.9. Sport had never come so close to being perfectly performed, and those of us fortunate enough to be present felt we were seeing one of the great moments in sporting history. What we could not have known – and would probably have refused to believe – was that there was better to come. We could not have comprehended it on that wonderful night in Helsinki.

GOLD INTO WHITE

After the gold costumes of
Mack and Mabel, we chose
the simplicity of white for
the circus act we devised
for Barnum, our free
dance for 1983. Sparkling
blue lapels and a cravat on
Chris and a sash around
Jayne's waist highlighted
the effect.

AN EMBRACE IN HELSINKI
Skating from the ice, the first bouquet and toy animal thrown on the ice already in our hands. After Barnum all nine judges at the World Championships in Helsinki awarded us sixes for artistic impression, a decision that earned a standing ovation for the judges as much as for us.

TRAPEZE ARTISTS ON ICE
The Barnum routine ran through the gamut of the circus, the trapeze artists, the clowns and the trombones of the band. In this scene Chris lifts Jayne in preparation for swinging her into a head over heels. Rival coaches questioned at the time whether it was within the rules, but the judges unanimously endorsed its legality.

KISS ME KATE
(Following pages) We performed *Kiss Me Kate* at a blues exhibition.

CHAPTER FOUR

1984

B•O•L•E•R•O

All that had gone before had in many ways been preparation for the Olympic Games, sport's ultimate challenge, so that all that they had achieved until now meant very little. Everything had to be new; only their reputation would go before them.

Twice they had worked their magic with a story. The audience was coming to expect it, but to try it a third time might be thought clichéd. They chose instead to create a mood using Ravel's *Bolero* and to take its slow crescendo to a dramatic conclusion. There was a thin story behind it, that of two lovers who could not live together but refused to be apart, leading them on a journey up a mountain from which they would hurl themselves to their deaths in a suicide pact. It was the beauty of the piece, the intensity of the emotion and the breathtaking finale as they threw themselves to the ice that grabbed the heart. The mysticism of Ravel's seventeen-minute composition was squeezed into four.

Half the world now seemed interested only in knowing whether they were as close off the ice as they appeared to be on it. Could any two people of the opposite sex look so deeply into each other's eyes with such fervour then just switch off at the rinkside? It was, says Jayne now, all a performance, play-acting, assuming a role and becoming it for four minutes – like any good actor does. 'We are making love for two minutes on the ice, and then we are just good friends', she was to say more recently of a blues dance.

But the public and media wanted more. Journalists beat a path to their training camp in Oberstdorf throughout the autumn of 1983 in pursuit of secret knowledge. Oh,

VICTORY AT THE EUROPEAN CHAMPIONSHIPS
Bolero was still to come, but Jayne is almost in tears and Chris is exultant as the judges award us six perfect sixes for artistic impression. We were disappointed that the Russian judge gave us only 5.6 for technique and placed us second behind our main challengers, the Soviet couple Natalya Bestemianova and Andrei Bukin. But the other skaters were more generous. Bestemianova even said that she could not free our performance from her thoughts for the rest of that day – and that is one of the highest compliments we could get.

yes, the ice dancing is all very interesting, they would say, but what about it? Can we hear wedding bells? All Jayne and Chris could think about was their one last lap of sporting honour. It looks so effortless, so serene, when it is performed but behind the aesthetic excellence are bruises, sweat and at times not a few tears.

EVEN THE SHARPNESS OF THEIR SKATES WAS CRITICAL, A FEW HUNDREDTHS OF A CENTIMETRE DIFFERENCE WAS DETECTABLE.

Their attention to detail could wreck a computer. Nothing can be left to chance. Jayne flew from Oberstdorf to London to get a piece of music right. Their costumer designer, Courtney Jones, skated behind them on the ice before sewing extra stitches into a blouse to improve its effect. Even the sharpness of their skates was critical, a few hundredths of a centimetre difference detectable when they skate at the limits.

But first came the choreography. The ISU chose a paso doble as the original for 1984 and threatened themselves with an avalanche of Españas. Chris and Jayne decided to take a bull-fighting theme in which Jayne would be the cape, ne the matador, and to capture the feeling Jones came up ith a costume that some consider his greatest creation.

It was Bolero, however, that caused controversy. There were lifts in it according to a Russian coach, Tatiana Tarassova, which broke the rule that the man's hand should not be raised above shoulder height. Not so, said Lawrence Demmy, chairman of the ISU's ice-dancing committee, adding sarcastically: 'I'm delighted to hear that after all these years the Russians have found their rule book.'

A few weeks before the Olympic Games, at the European Championships in Budapest, the Russians were still arguing the toss. Alexander Gorshkov, a former world champion, and the Russian judge Irina Absaliamova claimed that there were also faults in Torvill and Dean's original dance. When it came to marking it, Absaliamova gave it only 5.6 for technical merit, confirming that she believed something to be amiss with it.

She was spitting into the wind of change sweeping through ice dancing. It had long been the poor relation of figure skating, only arriving as an Olympic sport in 1976, and those concerned with its future well-being were not going to let a stone-hearted traditionalist spoil its most glorious hour. They were all in T & D's train, falling over themselves to set new records. In Budapest the two even achieved their ambition to score a six in a compulsory outside of Britain – and not just one. For their Westminster Waltz, three could find no fault with it, a mark never before awarded in an international championship. They were to do it again with the same dance at the Olympics.

IN BUDAPEST THE TWO EVEN ACHIEVED THEIR AMBITION TO SCORE A SIX IN A COMPULSORY – AND NOT JUST ONE.

When it came to Bolero, even Mrs Absaliamova's heart was touched. She was among all but one of the judges who gave it the stamp of artistic approval with sixes. The Britons regained the European title loaned temporarily a year earlier because of their enforced absence.

BRITISH HOPES

The first Olympic honour for Chris. He was chosen by the British team leaders to carry the flag at the opening ceremony of the 1984 Winter Games in Sarajevo, recognition that the British had hopes of a gold medal for us. Since we had won the European title against our principal rivals from the Soviet Union, interest focussed more on whether we would win even more sixes with Bolero than we did with Barnum.

So to Sarajevo. They trained for it in Oberstdorf and made their way in private to the games by train. Awaiting them was in full splendour the world's media, press conferences, photo opportunities, endless questions. But the only one that mattered was answered in the Zetra Stadium.

A formidable margin was put between them and the Russians in the compulsories, and increased when Torvill and Dean picked up four sixes in the original. Bolero did the rest. It was pure theatre. When they fell to the ice at the finish, the audience stood cheering for so long it was as though they were demanding an encore. Three sixes and six 5.9s for technical merit. Nine sixes for artistic impression – artistic perfection would be fairer. The gold, the Olympic title, was theirs.

It should have ended there, but they went through the motions of winning their fourth world title in Ottawa, Canada, the following month. Nobody remembers the 1984 World Championships now (except that the ice-machine broke down and kept television viewers wanting to see the performace live awake until the early hours of the morning). All that is forged in the memory is that single magnificent performance in Sarajevo.

THE BULLFIGHT

The paso doble was nominated for the original dance in the Olympic season, and we elected to present a scene from a bullfight: Chris was the matador, Jayne the cape. Her costume was a black cape with a gold fringe along the arms. When she spread out her arms, she revealed a flash of white from wrist to waist, like a cape being held in front of a bull. Though the choreography was planned first, the way Jayne's costume opened began to dictate changes that Chris would use to best effect.

THE PASO DOBLE

The conventional rhythm was 4/4 time, but we wanted to be different, so we decided to put a piece by Rimsky-Korsakov to 6/8 beat, a challenging task for a routine that had to be doubly squeezed into the two minutes allowed by the rules. We found Robert Stewart, a music teacher at a school in Surrey who conducted à church choir and had a background in the commercial musical world. We persuaded him to produce a score that turned out to be outstanding.

THE JOURNEY UP THE MOUNTAIN

The routine was the story of two lovers who have found each other but who know they cannot be together. So as one they climb a mountain, represented by the rising power of the music, until they reach the top and die together by throwing themselves off, a climax portrayed by a dramatic fall. We think it was perhaps the first time that a fall had been built into a skating programme.

FOUR MINUTES OF BOLERO

A sequence from Bolero, and this is just for starters. Ravel's music in full takes seventeen minutes to build its great crescendo, but the rules of ice dancing permitted us only four minutes. Incredibly, Robert Stewart managed to make the cuts without losing the effect, but to emphasize the climactic end the start had to be slow. Chris leans to take Jayne by the ankle and turn her over onto her skates. She turns, pleading with him to follow, finally bringing him to his feet as she skates away. We hoped the routine would be seen as a journey.

Jayne rolls over
Chris's back in a quick
move (right), while
the story's two lovers
move in complex criss-
crosses that represent
their inability to stay
together as they move
closer to the fate that
awaits them.

71

A PERFECT ROW OF SIXES
Bolero was a fitting finale to our amateur career. It is claimed that 100 million viewers around the world watched us in Sarajevo. We're glad we could leave behind perfect sixes – and a world record for ice skating at the Olympic Games.

CHAPTER FIVE

1 9 8 5 - 9 3

T*O*U*R*I*N*G

T*H*E

G*L*O*B*E

It was time to move on. Nothing could quite follow Bolero on a sporting stage, and it was best that they did not try. There were fresh pastures, new challenges, and they lay in the commercial world. It was time for Chris to cast off the chains of competition and let his creativity run riot. There was a living to be made, but it was the prize of artistic freedom that appealed, and even before the Olympic season ended they were bursting to expand their horizons.

First stops on the professional tour were Australia and New Zealand and the beginning of an association with two Australians, Graeme Murphy, who directed the Sydney Dance Company, and Andris Toppe, a teacher and former dancer who

WITHOUT RULES
Wherever we performed, audiences liked to see our most famous numbers. We must have been asked to do Bolero a thousand times. Our first professional tour with our own company of international skaters gave us the license to delve deeper into our creative resources. We came up with a succession of new showstopping numbers, seen by British fans when the tour called at Wembley Arena in London, for which we had a specially commissioned Big Top tent for the event. We performed the beautiful Song of India (above) and Shepherd's Song (preceding pages).

occasionally acted as Murphy's assistant. Murphy worked closely with Chris on his routines Song of India and Encounter. They toured in 1984 with a group of Russian skaters, several of whom had competed against them in the sporting arena, and they later appeared in the Royal Variety Performance in London. Chris had long been interested in other forms of dance, and his enthusiasm had been stimulated by working with a Hungarian ballet dancer at an earlier stage of his career, so working with Murphy, a renowned choreographer, brought out some of his best work.

Sport did not forget them immediately. At the end of the Olympic year BBC Television's viewers voted them Sports Personalities of the Year (they had been Team of the Year in 1983), and they won their first professional world ice dance championships in America, an event that did not demand rigorous training of compulsories and a victory that they were to repeat a year later.

By that time they had embarked on the first world tour in 1985. Murphy could not commit himself completely because of his responsibilities in Australia, but he agreed with Jayne and Chris that they needed a resident rehearsal and tour director. He recommended Toppe, a long-time friend who had been a dancer with Murphy in the Australian Ballet. So began an association that puts Toppe in a unique position to judge them as professional performers. 'In my experience as a dancer,' says Toppe, 'only Fonteyn and Nureyev had a comparable magic as a combination, but the partnerships of cinema's Bacall and Bogart, Taylor and Burton, and, of course, Astaire and Rogers are not far-fetched comparisons. One day, I have no doubt that the Torvill and Dean combination will be spoken of in similar terms. Their extraordinarily high degree of quality is first and foremost as a duo. Seen separately they are very good skaters, but it is when they are together that they have the capacity to flow seamlessly into and with each other's movement and body-line, that continually amazes me.'

'WHEN THEY ARE TOGETHER THEY HAVE THE CAPACITY TO FLOW SEAMLESSLY INTO EACH OTHER'S BODY-LINE.'

Toppe can speak from long experience of the many hours of hard work that go into creating what appears so effortless to their audiences. He calls it the 'daily slog', but he admits that his job is made so much easier by a 'miraculous osmosis'. 'They have a perfect understanding of each other's next move', he says.

Toppe believes that his personal contribution to their success lies largely in sharing with them his interest and enthusiasm for other art forms in music and theatre. Instructing them in cross-training, ballet, contemporary dance, gym-work, yoga and the Pilates system of non-aerobic exercising is designed to isolate and develop weaker muscles while lengthening and stretching stronger ones.

Toppe's introduction to the standards the two demand of each other came in their tour of 1985. 'Not just four minutes now but forty minutes at a time, sometimes eight times a week', says Chris of their professional performances. That demanded endless rehearsing of Chris's innovative choreography with the company of skaters they put together. Toppe's role in it is widely appreciated; less well understood is Jayne's contribution. 'Often it is underplayed or overlooked entirely', says Toppe. 'I have seen the results and the work processes, both when Jayne is present and when she has been absent. Believe me, there's a difference. Comparisons with artists and the muse or model who inspire them, such as Rodin with Camille Claudel, are not amiss in this connection.'

The success of the 1985 tour encouraged them to repeat it with a company of skaters from the Soviet Union in 1988. Other companies, such as the American Ice-Capades, called on their services as guest artists. There were television's demands to be satisfied as well, and a brilliant production called *Fire and Ice* was filmed for showing at Christmas in Britain in 1986.

Eventually the British television arts programme Omnibus, usually devoted to more obvious cultural activities, bestowed its approval on them with a documentary on their choreography, proving at least that they had not lost their ability to command a television audience: it attracted the highest viewing figures for the programme that season.

They never left the sporting scene entirely. The world professional championship was an occasional diversion for them. In 1990, with Toppe's help, they entered again and won, and that year they were chosen world professional skaters of the year, a great honour in a field strewn with wonderful skaters, many of whom had won Olympic and world honours in the amateur scene. Chris's involvement again with competition became even more marked when he began to choreograph competition pieces for a French-Canadian brother-sister combination, Paul and Isabelle Duschenay, who went on to win the world ice dance title in 1991 and the silver at the 1992 Olympic Games.

In 1992 Torvill and Dean prepared a new show for a tour of Britain, this time with a company of skaters recruited in the Ukraine. Weeks were spent in Kiev practising, and during the tour a television recording of it put the couple back on British television at Christmas. But by then, life for them had moved on. Sporting was beckoning them back, and this time as competitors. When they skated Bolero again – 'we must have been asked to do it thousands of times', says Chris – at a unique gathering of past Olympic champions in Boston, they knew that after ten long years there would be an encore: the 1994 Olympic Games.

A MONTH IN KIEV
During our month in Kiev, when we were rehearsing for our 1992 British Tour, we were struck by the beauty of the city's architecture.

THE WORLD TOUR

We were often asked to perform routines that we had had so much success with in amateur competition. With the atmospheric lighting available to us on the professional tour, we were able to take dances like Mack and Mabel and Paso Doble to new heights. In addition to England, our 1985 tour called on Australia, New Zealand, Canada and the United States.

81

TILT
We were delighted when the television programme Omnibus wanted to do a documentary on our choreography. The music for Tilt was a collaboration between English jazz saxophonist Andy Shepherd and Chris, and it allowed us to explore a whole new direction.

THE PLANETS SUITE
(Opposite) With our interpretation of Venus in the Planets Suite we wanted to create the illusion of Jane flying, which we achieved by having Chris, who was concealed within the cloak, lift Jane from underneath.

BOLERO UNCOVERED
(Below) We performed our 1985 tour all over the world, and in the finale we used voluminous cloaks to conceal our Bolero costumes. We always enjoyed the audience's reaction when they were revealed.

STORMY WEATHER

For our last British Tour, the theme of the finale was weather. Before the rainbow at the end, we decided to skate to the moody feel of Stormy Weather, very much as a parody of a couple's relationship.

MISSING

Performed in our 1988 World Tour, this piece was an idea conceived from reports we had read of people going missing in South America. With music by Incantation we tried to convey the searching of a brother and sister for their family. This is one of our favourite photographs, taken by a member of the audience.

HATTRICK

This was one of our favourite comic routines of the 1988 World Tour. It took hours of practice before we managed not to drop the hat. We spent two days with Lord Snowdon in what turned out to be a very enjoyable photographic shoot.

SKATER'S WALTZ
For the opening of our 1992 British Tour we chose the Skater's Waltz, a piece that recreated the feeling of the nineteenth century.

ENCOUNTER
A collaboration between Chris and Graeme Murphy, we performed Encounter in our 1985 tour and achieved our first victory with it at the 1984 World Professional Championships.

DRUM DUET
With music by Genesis, this was the last piece we choreographed before concentrating on our Olympic routine. Knowing we were returning to amateur competition, we tried to break every rule in the book.

WORKING IN KIEV
Our last commercial show toured Britain in 1992 with a company of Ukrainian dancers. Among the dances featuring the company were Over the Rainbow (below), Skater's Waltz and Hoedown (opposite) – a Country and Western Torvill and Dean style. Our rehearsal spaces (following pages) often showed signs of the former Soviet Union.

CHAPTER SIX

1993-94

L*E*T'*S

F*A*C*E T*H*E

M*U*S*I*C

A*N*D D*A*N*C*E

Chance brought them back into the sporting arena, just as it had brought them together all those years before in Nottingham. This time the invitation was to attend the one-hundredth anniversary celebration of the International Skating Union in Davos, Switzerland. Many of their old friends were there – the officials, judges and skaters of their earlier years – and the atmosphere was right. They were told that the ISU was changing its rule on the eligibility of skaters, and professionals would be welcomed for the first time.

Chris was interested. On the train journey from Davos, he mentioned it to Jayne. 'I thought he was drunk or something', she recalled. But the idea of

**PASSING THE
TORCH**
An old picture of
Jayne and Betty
Callaway, who says
that one day Jayne will
make an excellent
teacher. Already she
has helped Betty with
the training of
Britain's most promis-
ing young couple,
Justin Lanning and
Marika Humphreys,
and soon it may be
Jayne on the other
side of the boards.

one more Olympic challenge grew until it became irresistible. Ten months later their minds were made up, their diaries cleared and Betty Callaway and Bobby Thompson, were recruited again as coaches. Their eligibility was restored.

This time Jayne and Chris decided that they would prepare themselves at home. They accepted an offer to rent the Bladerunner Arena in Milton Keynes, and for four hours on weekdays and two hours on Sunday they were there, with practice overseen by Andris Toppe. Their physical fitness, honed by the professional demands of performing up to eight shows a week, was as good as ever, and having lifted Jayne as many as ninety times in an evening in their shows, Chris felt stronger than ten years earlier. Their competitive technique had to be polished again, but most of all the precision of the compulsories, which they had not performed since 1984, had to be mastered. 'It was like getting out a rusty bike and pedalling it again', said Chris. 'It was a six-month slog.'

There were other equally important details – not least a free dance different enough from Bolero so as not to be compared. Their choice for music was *Let's Face the Music and Dance,* a tune composed by Irving Berlin and made famous in a 1936 Hollywood movie starring the dance couple they very much admired: Fred Astaire and Ginger Rogers.

Berlin's score was re-arranged to fit into four minutes, and the arrangement was recorded with a full line-up of studio musicians. The whole operation – the rental of practice rinks, music, costumes and lost professional engagements – was estimated to cost them around £130,000, but if it was to be done, it was to be done well and no expense was to be spared in trying to re-create the sporting success they had achieved in the past.

Chris set to work choreographing a piece of ballroom dancing that would be as far removed from the passion of Bolero as it was possible to imagine, full of highly complex steps that led the eye towards the ice. Word had reached them from the ISU that they would appreciate a return to a more ballroom style from the theatrical legacy of Bolero, and Chris was happy to oblige. 'Very physical, very technical with lots of steps and plenty to see from the waist down', he described the free dance. 'We hope audiences will be moved by it in a light, show-bizzy way, not as they were

THE FREE DANCE WAS LIKE OLD TIMES: ALL NINE JUDGES GAVE SIXES FOR ARTISTIC IMPRESSION.

by Bolero'. All that remained was to offer it to their audience, and they did so on one Saturday afternoon in January 1994 at the British Championships in an arena in Sheffield.

There was very little doubt that they would win their seventh British title, but when the compulsories were completed, all doubt was gone. Their first marks in amateur competition since 1984 were not startling by their former standards, but they were far beyond anything the domestic competition could challenge. Their original dance, a new rumba routine set to sultry trumpet playing, was stunningly effective. Four judges awarded sixes for presentation.

The free dance was like old times: All nine judges gave sixes for artistic impression, and one gave them sixes for both sections. The audience that filled the arena loved the four-minute routine that ran through the lexicon of social dancing – waltz, foxtrot, tango and quickstep, with a few subtle elements of Mack and Mabel and Barnum thrown in. Flowers flooded the ice even before the judges gave their verdicts.

REPLAY
We're happy to say that after all those years the British Championships in Sheffield felt like a replay of the 1984 Olympics.

Reaction more widely was less enthusiastic. There were those who felt the routine was too clever, that its subtlety escaped the audience and that it did not succeed in creating an atmosphere. In many minds was an image of Bolero, and while admirers hardly dared to say it, there was disappointment. The couple themselves, while not admitting it, took the mood on board and made changes in the free dance for the European Championships in Copenhagen two weeks later, adding a few thrills to make the highlights more obvious.

The surprise in Copenhagen was the moderate marking of their compulsory dances. A Swiss judge awarded their paso doble only 5.2, an insulting mark lower than any they could remember. They were placed third, only rising to joint second with Oksana Gritschuk and Eugny

Platov after their blues but still behind Maya Usova and Alexandr Zhulin at the end of the first day.

The rumba was received with more appreciation. Two judges awarded sixes, and the couple won the section and became joint first with Usova and Zhulin. The free dance, worth fifty per cent of the marks, would be decisive. A fine-tuned routine with a cartwheel and two lifts added since Sheffield would decide whether they would go into the Olympic Games as favourites. Surprisingly, it did not find favour. Not one judge thought it was the best on offer, and it was the two Russian couples and skating's curious scoring system that conspired inadvertently to hand them their fourth European title.

Nobody immediately understood why the computer was placing Torvill and Dean first. After the marking of Grits-chuk and Platov, Usova and Zhulin were left with only two judges who still thought them best and three who placed them second. The world champions found themselves edged into third place overall because the majority of judges were voting for Torvill and Dean as their runners-up in the free section. Had a Ukrainian judge put a Finnish couple second in the free dance instead of fourth, Torvill and Dean would have received only a bronze medal.

Dean, seated on a bench in his subterranean bolt-hole, white-faced with anxiety, finally heard from a BBC producer linked by radio to one of his assistants that it would be a gold they collected. Hugs and kisses from everybody, but there was no disguising from the two principals that there was much more work to be done if they were to win again at the Olympic Games. 'We've been away ten years and this week felt like another ten', said Chris.

FACING THE MUSIC – AGAIN
The opening to our free programme was an interpretation of Irving Berlin's music *Let's Face the Music and Dance*, which Fred Astaire and Ginger Rogers made famous in the 1936 film *Follow the Fleet*. The steps were the most complicated we'd ever attempted – and fast: we reckon that the number of steps in all of Bolero could fit in the first minute of this routine.

1   2   3   4   5   6   7   8   9

6.0 6.0 6.0 6.0 6.0 6.0 6.0 6.0 6.0

THE SEVENTH TIME
If we missed one step, we'd miss them all – they come so quickly. But luckily we missed none at all, and we were astonished with our seventh British Championship. We were delighted to be selected as Britain's representatives at the European Championships in Copenhagen.

STEPPING OUT
After the joy of victory at the European Championships (above) we performed the rumba and the final section of Let's Face the Music and Dance for a gala exhibition (left) before setting out for Lillehammer, Norway, and the 1994 Winter Olympics.

CHAPTER SEVEN

1994

T·H·E
1·9·9·4
O·L·Y·M·P·I·C·S

They took a day off when they returned to Britain but it was to be their last respite before the Olympic Games in Lillehammer, Norway. The experience in Copenhagen had convinced them that they had misinterpreted what the skating world was looking to them to give it ten years on. If the ISU's technical committee for ice dancing wanted a return to a more strict ballroom style they had not communicated it to the judges. Chris knew that the routine they presented in Lillehammer would have to be more exciting. A true professional, he determined to give them what they wanted: the old Torvill and Dean, the innovators.

This was the greatest gamble of their lives. After

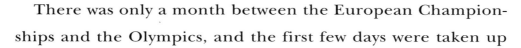

their achievements in 1984, they would have been justified in taking a well-earned retirement to bask in their status as two of the true sporting greats. Yet here they were, offering themselves again, this time against a sporting generation not even out of school when they were at their peak. It was never going to be easy, and now they knew how hard. Defeat was a distinct possibility.

There was only a month between the European Championships and the Olympics, and the first few days were taken up with creating new choreography. The BBC screened a fascinating documentary on their preparations, showing that perfection is not achieved without a struggle. Virtually the entire free dance was changed with bigger lifts.

Other adjustments helped capture the feel of the dance: Jayne's hair was cut shorter, her skirt was lengthened to give her a bit more height, and Chris abandoned the white tuxedo jacket he wore in Sheffield and Copenhagen. 'If Bolero was drama, this was going to be entertainment', said Betty Callaway. 'It took my breath away when I first saw it'. Changes were also made to the compulsories. During the ten years that Jane and Chris had been absent from amateur competition, other couples had taken to lifting their

BACK ON TRACK
The joy we felt on seeing the marks for the rumba rekindled our spirit after the disappointing compulsories.

free legs higher in the set patterns and putting more emphasis on arm movement. Jane and Chris made these alterations, but somewhat reluctantly, as they believed the compulsories should be judged on technique and edges.

THE RUMBA IS A DANCE OF LOVE, AND THEY CAPTURED THE INTENSITY OF A COUPLE WITH EYES ONLY FOR EACH OTHER.

But would they be ready? They delayed their departure for Norway until the Games were four days old, and then the pressure of public attention was diverted by the affair of the two American figure skaters Nancy Kerrigan and Tanya Harding. But there were enough eyes on them to notice when they practiced their new free routine for the first time in the Olympic Amphitheatre in Hamar that it looked rough at the edges. Chris slipped, and Jayne stumbled. It was left to Callaway to excuse them on the grounds that they had caught a skate in previous skaters' ruts, but the fears of their admirers were increased.

Concern deepened with the compulsory dances. They had been third on the first dance in Copenhagen but pulled up to joint second place after the second. This time they were third on the first and stayed third with the second. Chris stumbled slightly in one turn of their first dance to the music of the starlight waltz, and the judges hammered them unmercifully. They were awarded their worst marks in fourteen years. Their blues was greeted only fractionally more favourably, and the two Russian couples they had faced in Copenhagen led the way in joint first place. Compulsories are worth only twenty per cent of the total, so the Britons could afford nothing less than perfection in the remaining two routines.

The rumba is a dance of love, and the two captured the

intensity of a couple with eyes only for each other. 'We were in love for the two minutes we danced', said Jayne. 'We are still good friends. It's an act. We are taking a role when we perform, and we've been performing so much that we have learned to play all sorts of different characters.'

The rink at Hamar disappeared under a floral tribute to their brilliance. Bouquets tumbled down in such profusion that six small children filled their arms with them to clear the ice as 6,000 spectators stood to applaud. A Ukrainian and British judge awarded them sixes for presentation, with seven 5.9s, while their technique won them five 5.8s and four 5.9s.

The quality of their marks raised them to joint first place with Usova and Zhulin. They had only to win the free dance to win the gold, and the draw seemed to favour them. Usova and Zhulin would skate second of the last group of five, while Torvill and Dean skated immediately ahead of the last skaters, Gritschuk and Platov. Everything was prepared for a grand finale. Everything, as it turned out, except eight judges.

Their free programme was stunning. At least the audience thought so. Bouquets cascaded down – it seemed like Sarajevo all over again. Then came the marks. One six from the British judge Mary Parry, but from the rest nothing of great consequence. Usova and Zhulin's technical marks were better, and Gritschuk and Platov's would be better still. The crowd jeered, Jayne shed a tear, and after Chris commented that the audience were their judges they skated out to collect their Olympic bronze medals. It was not what they came back for.

The recriminations followed swiftly. Parry was carpeted by the referee for overmarking, while the world's media took it on themselves to accuse all concerned with prejudging the event. So horrified were the International Olympic

Committee at the bad publicity that the ISU was forced to call a media conference to explain, among other things, that when Chris finished with a grand flourish by sending Jayne over his head, he suffered an automatic deduction.

To end such illustrious careers with a slap on the wrist for a technical infraction that should have been pointed out by the judges who saw it in practice on three occasions showed an astonishing degree of ingratitude. Torvill and Dean's return, had once again raised ice dancing to new heights of public interest it had not known since their sporting retirements. Almost twenty-four million people watched their finale on television in Britain alone, a record for a sporting audience.

BEFORE THE STORM
In our first public rehearsal for the free dance we were nervous and not as sure-footed as we hoped to be on the night.

But this was how it was to end. Fittingly, they left their adoring audience in Norway with a performance that had won them the gold ten years earlier — an exhibition of Bolero at the gala that ended the Games' skating competition. A few days after their return to England, elated by the audience's response but disillusioned with the authorities that had eagerly welcomed them back a year earlier, Jane and Chris announced their withdrawal from the World Championships and left the amateur circuit for the freedom of the professional world once more.

STARLIGHT WALTZ AND BLUES

We will never forget the response from the audience the moment we entered the Olympic Arena again after ten years. Even for the compulsory dance we felt their support, and it lifted us throughout the games.

THE RUMBA

For the music we used a steamy arrangement by Cy Payne of *History of Love*, by Carlos Almaran. We had used another arrangement back in 1982 as an exhibition piece, and when it was decided that the rumba was to be the original dance for this year, we had no hesitation in deciding to use this piece again, but with new choreography.

A NEW FAVOURITE

Many people have said to us to us that our 1984 paso doble was their favourite OSP dance, now it seems our rumba is the favourite original dance.

EXHAUSTED AND ELATED

With our new free dance it took every ounce of our energy to perform at what we believed was our best level. With the added lifts, jumps and 'tricks' the stamina needed to execute all the intricate footwork was tremendous, but again the audience was with us every step of the way.

By the time we finished the four-minute routine, we were exhausted and elated. As we have been quoted as saying since the games, the audience that night around the world, we felt, were our judges.

LAST DANCE
At the exhibition gala at the Lillehammer Olympics we dedicated our performance of Bolero to the people of Sarajevo. It seems incredible to us that ten years has passed since we last skated Bolero in amateur competition. Whatever our future holds, we hope to be skating for as long as we are physically able. In the years ahead we hope to bring as much pleasure to the audience as they have given us in support.

NO REGRETS
Naturally we hoped to be featured on the medal-winner's rostrum. We achieved our aim and after ten years' absence from amateur competition people have said that winning a bronze medal was remarkable. Maybe it's not the position we had hoped for, but we don't regret making our return to amateur competition.

COMPETITION RECORD

1976   1st Sheffield Trophy
            1st Northern championship
            1st St Gervais
            2nd Oberstdorf
            4th British championship

1977   1st Oberstdorf
            3rd British championship

1978   9th European championship, Strasbourg
            11th World championship, Ottawa
            1st John Davis Trophy
            1st British championship (first 6.0)

1979   6th European championship, Zagreb
            8th World Championship, Vienna
            2nd Rotary Watches competition, Richmond
            1st British Championship
            2nd NHK competition, Tokyo

1980   4th European championship, Gothenburg
            5th Olympic Games, Lake Placid
            4th World championship, Dortmund
            1st St Ivel competition, Richmond
            1st British championship

1981   1st European championship, Innsbruck
            1st World championship, Hartford
            1st St Ivel competition, Richmond
            1st British championship

1982   1st European championship, Lyons
            1st World championship, Copenhagen
            1st British championship

1983   1st World championship, Helsinki

1984   1st European championship, Budapest
            1st Olympic Games, Sarajevo
            1st World championship, Ottawa, Canada

1994   1st British championship, Sheffield
            1st European championship, Copenhagen
            3rd Olympic Games, Lillehammer, Norway

First published in Great Britain in 1994 by
George Weidenfeld and Nicolson Ltd
The Orion Publishing Group
Orion House
5 Upper St Martin's Lane
London WC2H 9EA

Edited by Lucas Dietrich
Designed by Bradbury and Williams
Litho origination by Pixel Colour Ltd, London
Printed and bound by Butler & Tanner Ltd, Frome and London

A cataloguing-in-publication record for this book is available from
the British Library.

PICTURE CREDITS
All photographs are by Bob Martin or Allsport, except on the following pages: 84 (top left): David Muscroft; 84 (bottom left): Steve
Smith; 84 (right): Snowdon; 85 (bottom): Trevor Leighton;
87 (top): Gerrard Vandystadt

ACKNOWLEDGEMENTS
The publishers would like to thank all those who helped in putting
this book together so quickly, and particularly to Debbie Turner,
who was instrumental in ensuring the book's accuracy.